And Then There's **GRACE**

Lindsay Williams

And Then There's Grace

ISBN: 9798308064312
Imprint: Independently published

©2025

All scriptures use from the KJV unless otherwise noted

Definitions used from: Merriam-Webster

GRACE:

Unmerited divine assistance given to humans for their regeneration or sanctification

Approval; Favor

And Then There's Grace

Table of Contents:

Introduction

Day 1: Amazing Grace

Day 2: Thankful for Grace

Day 3: To God be the Glory

Day 4: It's All God

Day 5: Sufficiency

Day 6: Blessed Assurance

Day 7: Grace Teaches

Day 8: Grace Wins

Day 9: Grace Extended

Day 10: Don't Abuse Grace

Day 11: I Won't Waste His Grace

Day 12: Grace Births Humility

Day 13: Grace is a Blessing

Day 14: Enjoy the Liberty

Day 15: Presentation is Everything

Day 16: More Grace

Day 17: Grace Out Loud

Day 18: Work Your Grace

Day 19: Grace Gift, Faith Activated

Day 20: Grace Adds

Day 21: Grace for Promises

Introduction

After writing the Mercy First book and devotional, I knew I wanted to write something about grace. I believe that the two are parallel to each other and there needs to be clear understanding on how they work and how we can use them in our daily lives.

I pray that as you dive into this devotional over these next 21 days, that you keep this word in mind, UNDESERVED. Remembering that this GRACE that you receive is not something you earned or deserve but God gives because of His Love for you. I pray that you not only learn about grace, but that you develop a deeper appreciation for God's grace towards you. I also pray that it challenges you to be an extender of grace to others.

And Then There's Grace

Day 1

Amazing Grace

1 Peter 5:10 KJV

"But the God of all grace, who hath called us unto his eternal glory by Christ Jesus, after that ye have suffered a while, make you perfect, stablish, strengthen, settle you."

When I think of grace, the word Amazing comes to mind. To serve a God that is faithful towards us, to give us things that we don't deserve sounds AMAZING to me.

The scripture says that "after we suffered a while, He makes us perfect, stablishes us, strengthens us and settles us. The truth is, we deserve the opposite, we deserve death, but Jesus put Himself in our place. He died for our sins and put us back in right standings with Him and makes grace available to us. That should make you eternally grateful and every time you receive His grace, you should say:

Lord your grace is AMAZING!!!

Today's Reflection:

Take a few moments and write out a time when you experienced God's grace and it made you say, AMAZING GRACE!!!

And Then There's Grace

And Then There's Grace

Day 2

Thankful for Grace

1 Timothy 1:13-14 NIV

"Even though I was once a blasphemer and a persecutor and a violent man, I was shown mercy because I acted in ignorance and unbelief. The grace of our Lord was poured out on me abundantly, along with the faith and love that are in Christ Jesus."

If you don't know Paul's story, He was once a man named Saul and he was not a good man. He was well educated, spoke fourteen different languages, well accomplished but he didn't know God. He persecuted those that loved God and had many believers killed. But, he had his Damascus road experience where God got his attention and introduced Himself to Saul, struck him blind for three days and changed his name from Saul to Paul.

If you read the full story of Paul's conversion in Acts 9:1-19, you can see God's grace in action. I'm sure God was tired of Saul persecuting His children and as a father he stepped in. Instead of killing him off, which he could have done, He showed His grace and changed his life, his name, and his identity.

In this verse, Paul is remembering that and he's THANKFUL. I feel sometimes we easily forget that it was God and without Him we are nothing. We feel entitled to grace because God freely gives it, but we are not entitled to grace. Every time we experience God's grace or we take a look back and remember how great God has been/and is to us it should spark a strong spirit of thankfulness.

Today's Reflection:

Take a moment today and think about how far you've come. Ask yourself where would I be without God's grace on my life. Then write out expressions of THANKSGIVING.

And Then There's Grace

And Then There's Grace

Day 3

To God be the Glory

2 Peter 3:18 AMP

"but grow [spiritually mature] in the grace and knowledge of our Lord and Savior Jesus Christ. To Him be glory (honor, majesty, splendor), both now and to the day of eternity. Amen."

As we have given God thanks for His grace being active in our lives, we must be reminded to give ALL GLORY back to God. When we experience success and victories it's easy to become addicted to the compliments and praise. Yes it feels good to be recognized and acknowledged but we as recipients of grace we have to remember that everything we accomplish is because of God.

Psalm 121:1-2
"I will lift up mine eyes to the hills from whence cometh my help. My help cometh from the Lord, which made heaven and earth."

Don't forget where your help comes from. Don't forget that it was the Lord that gifted you with the knowledge to do what you do. I believe this saying is thrown around like a cliche now but it needs to be redefined and become sacred for believers: To God Be the Glory.

Today's Reflection:

As you think about every accomplishment, every promotion, every successful moment in your life, take a few moments and truly give God ALL THE GLORY.

And Then There's Grace

And Then There's Grace

Day 4

It's All God

Ephesians 2:8-10 NLT

"God saved you by his grace when you believed. And you can't take credit for this; it is a gift from God. Salvation is not a reward for the good things we have done, so none of us can boast about it. For we are God's masterpiece. He has created us anew in Christ Jesus, so we can do the good things he planned for us long ago."

As stated on yesterday, All Glory Belongs to God. I think for some, you may be okay with saying "To God be the Glory" in your private time but God needs you to make it known to the world that you give Him all the credit for what He's done and for what He is doing in your life.

We see a lot of athletes after a good game and the commentators say, "you had a good game today" or how were you all able to come back and get the win" many athletes respond "I would like to give honor to God", or "it was with the help of my savior Jesus Christ". Many people don't like when they respond like that, many criticize and say they're doing too much but we as believers and recipients of grace should make it a daily practice to say IT'S ALL GOD!!!

God created us with purpose and for purpose. And when we are living and walking in our purpose we must remember that it's God that has given us the ability. It is because of God that I do what I do. The Bible says it best in Acts 18:28 *"for in him we live, and move, and have our being"*.

Today's Reflection:

Take some time today, write out some accomplishments and goals you were able to achieve, then remind yourself in all cap letters IT'S ALL GOD!!!

And Then There's Grace

And Then There's Grace

And Then There's Grace

Day 5

Sufficiency

2 Corinthians 12:9 KJV

"And he said unto me, My grace is sufficient for thee: for my strength is made perfect in weakness. Most gladly therefore will I rather glory in my infirmities, that the power of Christ may rest upon me."

This is one of my favorite scriptures in the Bible. Paul was faced with a challenge and he asked God three times to remove the thorn that was sent as he stated to keep him humble. God wanted him to learn to trust Him while going through. I know, I know, we hate hearing that phrase "going through" but the thing is we get to know God much more by going through than if He just comes and gets us out of trouble.

God tells Paul "my grace is sufficient". A simple definition for sufficient is having enough. The good news for you today is God has MORE THAN ENOUGH GRACE FOR YOU!!! You will never try to withdraw grace and get insufficient funds. You don't serve a God that is deficient in anything He offers or gives. You can have total trust in God and His ability to have a bountiful supply of grace for you.

Today's Reflection:

Take a moment today and reflect on God's grace in your life and His sufficiency in your life.

And Then There's Grace

And Then There's Grace

And Then There's Grace

Day 6

Blessed Assurance

Titus 3:7 KJV

"that being justified by his grace, we should be made heirs according to the hope of eternal life."

We are living in a world with so much helplessness, hopelessness, and uncertainty. There is so much chaos, trouble, and loss of life that it can leave you depressed and hopeless.

One thing I love about God is that He is full of hope. He constantly reminds us in His word in Hebrews 13:5 "I will never leave you, nor forsake you". This promise is not just for things, but to know that you have a savior that vows to be with you no matter what is something we should take comfort in.

With this same assurance, we have hope that because Jesus saved us and we have been justified by grace we have eternal life. Let that be your blessed assurance today, that no matter what happens in this world, this world is not your home. The grace that Jesus gives, guarantees you eternal life.

Today's Reflection:

Take today to meditate on the promises of God and the assurance that you have in Him. Write in faith what you're believing God for.

And Then There's Grace

And Then There's Grace

Day 7

Grace Teaches

Titus 2:11-13 AMP

"For the [remarkable, undeserved] grace of God that brings salvation has appeared to all men. It teaches us to reject ungodliness and worldly (immoral) desires, and to live sensible, upright, and godly lives [with a purpose that reflect spiritual maturity] in this present age, awaiting and confidently expecting the [fulfillment of our] blessed hope and the glorious appearing of our great God and Savior, Christ Jesus, "

And Then There's Grace

Being a recipient of grace should not turn you into someone that is prideful, arrogant, and hard to live with. It should be the total opposite. Receiving grace from God should make you humble, and easy to get along with. Remember at the beginning, I said as you journey through this devotional to remember the word UNDESERVED, here is where it comes into play.

When you realize that anything God does for you He doesn't have to do; any time you see grace at work in your life where God is providing opportunities and growth, it is imperative that we show someone else the way. Daily we should be growing in grace and apart of us growing and becoming is to teach someone else how to grow and become.

Grace is not given to us for us to be selfish. I believe we are called to not just be recipients of grace but to be givers of grace. As we give grace, we should show others what it looks like to grow in grace and how to accept grace from the Father.

Allow the grace of God to teach you how to live, reject sin, and embrace a holy lifestyle as the scripture for the day states and in doing that as you learn, teach someone else.

Today's Reflection:

Today, meditate on what grace has taught you, what you feel you have yet to learn. Then write what areas you feel you can teach someone else and help them on their grace journey.

And Then There's Grace

And Then There's Grace

Day 8

Grace Wins

Romans 5:20 KJV

"Moreover the law entered, that the offence might abound. But where sin abounded, grace did much more abound: "

And Then There's Grace

In this scripture, using my spiritual imagination I can see grace and sin in a fight for our soul. David wrote in Psalm 51:5 "Behold, I was shapen in iniquity; And in sin did my mother conceive me." The contemporary English version says, "I have sinned and done wrong since the day I was born."

For many sin has become natural so much so that you see no reason to change. Some have adopted the "this is just who I am" attitude and refuse to even be open to change. Sin only has the power over you that YOU allow it to have. There are many that are bound by the power of Satan, but please know that Grace is fighting for you!!! Grace never loses!!!!

Today's scripture says where sin abounded, grace much more abounds. God has a way of escape for you. You can change and become a new creature in Jesus. Grace will win, but you have to accept it. Take the grace!!

Today's Reflection:

Today, meditate and write down a time where you've seen God's grace win and prevail in your life.

And Then There's Grace

And Then There's Grace

Day 9

Grace Extended

Hebrews 12:15 AMP

"See to it that no one falls short of God's grace; that no root of resentment springs up and causes trouble, and by it many be defiled;"

Hebrews 12:15 CEV

"Make sure no one misses out on God's wonderful kindness. Don't let anyone become bitter and cause trouble for the rest of you."

And Then There's Grace

For most of this journey I have talked about how to be a recipient of grace. Now it's time to talk about being a GIVER of grace. Grace is that gift that we have to be willing to share with others, because I believe it was not meant for us to keep to ourselves and it should be something that we want everyone to have.

It takes discipline to give something away that you want and need for yourself. It takes courage to show someone grace when they have done something to you that offended you or caused harm or confusion. In order to be successful at being a Grace Giver is to remember how much grace God gives you, remember how many times you fell and instead of death, God gave life.

Take a look at today's scripture, it is our duty to make sure others get to experience God's grace. We should not allow resentment and confusion to be amongst us. It does not mean that we should not hold people accountable but it does mean that we should have a spirit of compassion and understanding and to be able to show God's love in the earth.

My prayer for you today is that God develops a desire in you for you to be a Grace Giver.

Today's Reflection:

Take today to write out ways that you can be a Grace Giver.

And Then There's Grace

And Then There's Grace

Day 10

Don't Abuse Grace

Romans 6:1-2 KJV

"What shall we say then? Shall we continue in sin, that grace may abound? God forbid. How shall we, that are dead to sin, live any longer therein?"

My father and Pastor always says *"Just because you can do a thing doesn't mean that you should."* That can be applied to any area of life and especially as it relates to grace. There are those that feel that they are the only ones that deserve grace, and there are others that feel that because God shows them grace instead of punishment that they can do anything they want because Grace will cover.

Paul clearly tells us that we should not keeping sinning and think that we're going to have grace at the same time. On a previous day we talked about Grace wins because where sin is grace abounds more; but if we continue to choose sin and not grace, grace will not abound.

Holiness is still a requirement to truly have the grace of God to stay active in your life. Never take advantage of God's grace to still fulfill the lust of the flesh. Please do not feel that you are getting by just because you haven't been punished yet.

Today's Reflection:

Pray and meditate today on times where you may have chosen your desires over grace, take a moment to write a prayer of repentance. Then pray for God to help you be holy even in decision making, pray that He helps you be sober in your mind and that you have the discipline to not abuse God's grace.

And Then There's Grace

And Then There's Grace

And Then There's Grace

Day 11

I Won't Waste His Grace

1 Corinthians 15:10 CEV

"But God treated me with undeserved grace! He made me what I am, and his grace wasn't wasted. I worked much harder than any of the other apostles, although it was really God's grace at work and not me."

And Then There's Grace

When you realize how invaluable grace is, you will never waste it. Paul knew better than anyone how valuable God's grace was in his life. He never forgot where God brought him from and how he was a terrible sinner that killed people and hated God but God still saved him and gave him grace instead of death, he had to live it out, he had to be grateful and he could not allow it to go to waste.

If you are like me, you hate to see food or anything being wasted. You know the value of it, you know someone took time to prepare and serve it. You hate to see the work involved not recognized. It should be the same way with God's grace. When you know what God has brought you out of and saved you from, when you remember His sacrifice for you on Calvary and that even though you don't deserve it, He still shows it daily you will not want to waste it.

Do what you have to do to show God that you appreciate Him for all He has done and is doing for you. Do all you can to serve Him in spirit and truth. Never forget that if it was not for God's grace you will not be who and what you are today.

Today's Reflection:

Take some time today to remember God's faithfulness towards you even when you were not faithful to Him. Let Him know that you will not take advantage and waste His investment in you.

And Then There's Grace

And Then There's Grace

Day 12

And Then There's Grace

Grace Births Humility

Romans 12:3 CEV

"I realize God has treated me with undeserved grace, and so I tell each of you not to think you are better than you really are. Use good sense and measure yourself by the amount of faith that God has given you."

There is nothing worse than receiving something that you don't deserve and you get arrogant about it. Arrogance should not be a trait among believers. In this text, Paul is saying don't think you are better than the next person, don't become conceited. Being a recipient of Grace should make you humble and appreciative.

In this season I believe that God is birthing a level of humility within us and He wants us to demonstrate what that looks like in the earth. People need to see how you are supposed to carry yourself being a recipient of grace.

Please remember that being humble is not outdated but it's a mandate for believers. God said in His word in James 4:6 *"But he giveth more grace. Wherefore he saith, God resisteth the proud, but giveth grace unto the humble."*

So in order to have God's grace active in your life, you must be humble.

Today's Reflection:

Pray today that God will work within you and birth a spirit of humility so that you can house God's grace.

And Then There's Grace

And Then There's Grace

Day 13

Grace is a Blessing

Numbers 6:24-25 KJV

"The LORD bless thee, and keep thee: The LORD make his face shine upon thee, and be gracious unto thee: "

When you have God's grace activated in your life and you can see it at work it is a TRUE BLESSING!!!

Always remember that there should be nothing that can substitute the grace of God in your life, there should be nothing that can substitute the light of the Lord shining bright in your life. Those things should be a non-negotiable.

Value the blessing of God's grace. Hold it like you would a newborn baby, secure it like you do the fine china, act as if you could lose it at any given moment. You never want to know what life is like without God's grace.

Today's Reflection:

Take a moment today to reflect on God's grace in your life and how much of a blessing it is to you. How much do you value that blessing?

And Then There's Grace

And Then There's Grace

Day 14

Enjoy the Liberty

Romans 6:14 GNT

"Sin must not be your master; for you do not live under law but under God's grace."

I love this facet of God's grace, it is liberating!!! Grace is not just about having favor to get "stuff" but it's all about being FREE from the chains of sin and bondage. We should never forget that purpose. Paul said in today's scripture that sin must not be your master because you're not under the law anymore, you're under GRACE.

Don't allow the enemy to keep you in bondage, neither your mind in bondage. I feel many times when we get saved, or delivered from a situation the devil doesn't mind the confession but he does mind when you make up your mind to break free and actually walk in deliverance. Deliverance is a decision and trust me the enemy does not want you to make that decision to not just confess but to accept God's grace to free you.

God doesn't want you to be free and you not enjoy it. Allow the liberating power of God's grace to break off the guilt and shame. The Bible says in Romans 8:1 "There is therefore now no condemnation to them which are in Christ Jesus, who walk not after the flesh, but after the Spirit."

Your life in Christ is meant to be enjoyed. You are free. You are loved. You are not there anymore. Embrace and enjoy your liberty in Christ.

Today's Reflection:

Meditate on your freedom today.

And Then There's Grace

And Then There's Grace

Day 15

Presentation is Everything

Colossians 4:5-6 MSG

"Use your heads as you live and work among outsiders. Don't miss a trick. Make the most of every opportunity. Be gracious in your speech. The goal is to bring out the best in others in a conversation, not put them down, not cut them out."

Have you ever wanted to be apart of a project but the details was not clear and things just seemed to be thrown together? Have you ever been apart of a program and the presenter did not capture your attention? Have you ever been in a service and the preacher's sermon told you everything you did wrong but didn't offer hope or solutions for change?

PRESENTATION IS EVERYTHING!!!!

How we present to people in the marketplace will determine if we get the client or if they choose someone else. The same is in the spirit, how we present Christ will determine rather people turn to Him or away from Him. Yes the gospel must be preached but if we are constantly sending everyone to hell, when are we telling them about the power of mercy, grace, redemption and hope. We must present with GRACE!! The Bible says in Proverbs 11:30 KJV "The fruit of the righteous is a tree of life; And he that winneth souls is wise." The CEV version says "And if you act wisely, others will follow you".

Make sure the way you present Jesus will make someone want to be saved. Make sure the way you live your life will make someone want to follow you. Truth is, we are living epistles, we are the blueprint, we will be the only Jesus some will see. And we must make our presentation attractive, convicting, compelling. We must speak to the spirit in the person, speak life, speak change. We must bring out the best in everyone around us. People should always leave our presence BETTER than they were when they came.

Today's Reflection:

Self-reflect on how is your presentation to others about your walk with God? Do you show His grace?

And Then There's Grace

And Then There's Grace

Day 16

More Grace

James 4:6 AMP

"But He gives us more and more grace [through the power of the Holy Spirit to defy sin and live an obedient life that reflects both our faith and our gratitude for our salvation]. Therefore, it says, "God is opposed to the proud and haughty, but [continually] gives [the gift of] grace to the humble [who turn away from self-righteousness]."

And Then There's Grace

There is nothing wrong with a healthy desire to have more of anything. Many have been made to feel that wanting more is being greedy and that you're not humble. I believe that keeping that mindset is the breeding ground for complacency. Never lose your desire for more and the passion to go after it.

When it comes to wanting more as it relates to Grace, it shouldn't be for show and to rack up "things". The desire for more grace should be so that you will gain strength through the spirit to defy sin and live an obedient life. We should want more grace so that we can turn away from self-righteousness and live humbly before God. The scripture says "he continually gives grace to the humble." We should want more grace so that we can extend grace to others as God extends it to us.

As long as your motives are pure before God, pursue MORE GRACE!!!!

Today's Reflection:

How you would benefit from the more from God?

And Then There's Grace

And Then There's Grace

Day 17

Grace Out Loud

Hebrews 4:16 KJV

"Let us therefore come boldly unto the throne of grace, that we may obtain mercy, and find grace to help in time of need."

And Then There's Grace

We have learned a lot about grace. Today's lesson is vital to you and your growth in God. BE BOLD!!! Grace is something undeserved, but we also learned that grace is something we should pursue. Anything you are going after you cannot be afraid to be bold and be loud. The Bible tells us in today's scripture to COME BOLDLY before the throne of grace that you may obtain mercy AND find grace to help in time of need.

My mother always tell me to never be afraid to ask her for anything I need. That's easier said than done because sometimes I revert back to the little girl and I get nervous. God is the same way, He does not want us to be afraid to come to Him about anything we need, but that can be a little intimidating coming before a mighty God with what we think is a minor thing when there are other things he could be doing. God wants you to know today your needs are important to Him, don't come quiet and timidly but come boldly, come loud.

Don't be afraid to grace out loud. As you are a recipient, be grateful for it and as a giver of it, show it out loud. Grace is something we all should be loud about.

Today's reflection:

How can I grace out loud as a recipient and a giver of grace?

And Then There's Grace

And Then There's Grace

Day 18

Work Your Grace

Ephesians 4:7 KJV

"But unto every one of us is given grace according to the measure of the gift of Christ."

And Then There's Grace

Here we are to the facet of grace where we have to get to work!! When we receive God's grace, we receive an assignment that we must carry out. We must seek the Lord to find out what is the grace on my life and when we get the answer, we must work our grace!!!

We must be careful to not covet another person's grace, even if their grace is similar to ours. Everyone is not called to the pulpit or to pastor a church. Some are called to lead in the marketplace, some are called to healthcare, some are graced for education , some are graced for military service but whatever you are graced for WORK YOUR GRACE!!!

Remember that someone is waiting on you to work YOUR grace, someone is going to come to Jesus because you're working YOUR grace. Someone will gain the confidence to work their grace because you are working YOUR GRACE. Nobody else will be able to do what YOU are graced to do, so let's get busy!!!

Today's Reflection:

Do I know what I have been graced to do? How can I work my Grace?

And Then There's Grace

And Then There's Grace

Day 19

Grace Gift, Faith Activated

Romans 12:6 TPT

"God's marvelous grace imparts to each one of us varying gifts. So if God has given you the grace-gift of prophecy, activate your gift by using the proportion of faith you have to prophesy."

Not only do we have to work our grace, the way we activate the gift is through our faith. It takes faith to do anything for God. We have to believe that He called us, we have to believe that we can do what He called us to do and when we have moments of uncertainty, we have to believe that God knows what we don't.

When we give gifts around the holidays, most of the toys say "batteries not included". Spiritually, we already have the gift within us, FAITH is the batteries that's not included but vital to bring the gift alive. You got to buy the batteries for the gift to work and you must have the faith to wake up and activate the grace gift that's on your life.

I pray that as you're discovering what your grace is, that your faith is stirred and activated to bring your grace gift alive so that you can do all that God has called you to do.

Today's Reflection:

Do I have the batteries (Faith) to fully operate my grace gift? Is my faith at a level to carry my grace gift?

And Then There's Grace

And Then There's Grace

Day 20

Grace Adds

John 1:16 CEV

"Because of all that the Son is, we have been given one blessing after another."

Grace is a great addition to your life and walk with God. It adds accountability, freedom, and it's activated by faith. One thing that grace doesn't do is take anything necessary away from you; it does remove things that you don't need and brings change that you do need. If grace is not adding to your life something is wrong.

The scripture says "because of all that Jesus is (the Son), we have been given one blessing after another". Embrace it. Don't be afraid of it. Being a recipient of God's grace has benefits and we should never be afraid to use our benefits to its full advantage.

As you grow in grace, allow grace to add to your life everything that you need or feel deficient in. We learned in one of the previous days that God's grace is sufficient and His strength is made perfect in our weakness.

Today's Reflection:

Think about how you have grown in grace and the areas where God's grace can add to your life.

And Then There's Grace

And Then There's Grace

Day 21

Grace for Promises

Isaiah 1:19 KJV

"If ye be willing and obedient, ye shall eat the good of the land:"

Every good father wants their children to succeed and go beyond what they have done. They will always try to set their children up for success rather it be to inherit the family business or helping them connect with people that are in the field they want to be in. There is nothing wrong with that. I strongly believe God sets us up the same way. It does not come without some requirements and instructions.

Being willing and obedient opens up the kind of grace that allows us to eat the good of the land. God is very clear on that. The stipulation is "IF" because many won't be and they won't be able to reap that benefit. God's grace positions us to receive His promises but the question is will we do our part?

Our Father has great hopes for us, and He will do His part to place us where we need to be to get them but we must be willing to do our part and obey. There are a lot of promises in His word that God is releasing a grace upon us for us to receive, but we as His children must be willing to do the work to receive the grace for His promises to be released to us.

Today's Reflection:

Are you willing to follow in your Father's guidance to receive the grace for His promises to be released to you? If you have some reservations, what's hindering you?

And Then There's Grace

And Then There's Grace

I hope that you have grown in these 21 days. I pray that you have a better understanding and a deeper appreciation of the role that grace plays in your life. As you continue to grow in grace that you position yourself to be a grace recipient and more importantly become a grace giver.

Grace is a vital and valuable asset to every believer. My hope is that you never forget that even though grace is freely given by God it is undeserved by us and since He chooses to extend grace to us that we will never lose our appreciation for it being at work in our lives.

Made in the USA
Columbia, SC
25 February 2025